Above:
St. Edwards crown, believed to have been fashioned from that of King Edward, the Saxon monarch, has been used at every coronation since 1660.

Above right:
The tranquil landscape of the north Somerset coast provides fertile grazing land for sheep.

Right:
The enormous sarsen blocks, at the centre of Stonehenge each weigh 50 tons. The mortice and tenon that attached the upright to the horizontal stones can still be seen.

Far right:
One of the most magnificent mansions in the country, Chatsworth was built at the end of the 17th century in classical style.

Book of Treasures

HAMLYN

The Cheapside Hoard, buried during the plague epidemic of 1603, is the best collection of English jewellery of the period outside that belonging to the Crown.

First published in 1985 by
The Hamlyn Publishing Group Limited
Bridge House, 69 London Road,
Twickenham, Middlesex, England.
© The Hamlyn Publishing Group
Limited

ISBN 0 600 50179 5

Printed in Spain

Larsa D. L. TF. 202 - 1985

Contents

Introduction

ritain's treasures have been harvested from many sources. From Prehistoric times, when the British Isles and France were joined by a strip of ice-covered land, waves of colonisers have crossed over to our shores, mixing with the indigenous population and spreading new customs and ideas.

Thus Stonehenge, still wreathed in mystery as it stands forbidding on Salisbury Plain, was begun two and a half thousand years before the birth of Christ and added to by successive settlers. The gold metalwork from the Sutton Hoo treasure was excavated from the Anglo-Saxon ship burial of King Raedwald. Four centuries earlier, Pevensey castle in Sussex had been built by the Romans as a defence against these Saxon invaders and was in turn reconstructed by the Normans after the Conquest of 1066 to protect their new island kingdom from attack.

From this date, Britain, so frequently the prey of marauders and invaders, began slowly to forge her nationhood until she became the aggressor. Her strength lay in her naval power, encouraged by such commanders as Drake and Nelson, fostering the creation of the British Empire, which by the reign of Queen Victoria was greater than that of Rome in her heyday. British ships sailed the world pirating Spanish treasure, fighting the French and exploring the South Seas. Wealth and treasure flooded back to the mother country while contact with foreign courts and lands encouraged the creation of splendid buildings, of cathedrals and palaces, such as York Minster and Chatsworth.

Our galleries and stately homes are full of great works by foreign artists. However, the brilliance of the European Masters should not blind us to the masterworks of our native-born artists such as Turner and Constable. The latter in particular loved his native Britain, painting fields, trees and animals with genius and delight. A Constable is now beyond the reach of anyone but a millionaire and yet his paintings were inspired by what is perhaps the greatest treasure Britain has to offer – her very fabric – the Devon hills, the chalk cliff face of the Kent and Sussex coast, the grandeur and magnificence of the Scottish lochs – the list is endless in its variety. And here, paradoxically, is treasure trove that we can all enjoy, that we do not own and yet which belongs to us all.

Yet still beneath the soil are hidden treasures, perhaps a coin dropped by a careless legionary patrolling a lonely stretch of Hadrians Wall or a cache of jewels concealed by a victim of the plague. Farmers and building contractors are frequently turning up objects or evidence of earlier settlement in their working day, and though this treasure may often seem worthless, to an archaeologist every piece of evidence is important in order to create a mosaic of detail and thus attempt to discern the pattern of history.

So our treasures are all around us – in art galleries and museums, in our magnificent buildings, in the countryside itself, perhaps still concealed under the soil. These treasures are valuable in themselves and precious to us because they make up a whole that is greater than the sum of its parts – Our Heritage.

Opposite:
A view of Stoke by Nayland, a Suffolk farming village, on a glorious late summer's afternoon.

Chapter One

"This Sceptr'd Isle"

lbion was an ancient name for the British Isles, derived from the Latin 'albus' meaning 'white' because, to a colonist from Europe, the first sight of her shores was the gleam of white rock. The white cliffs of England were the result of millions of years of sediment accumulating on the floor of the ocean and raised by earth movements. Indeed Britain today is the result of enormous and varied geological changes. The Pennines, for example, were created as a result of volcanic activity as molten rock forced itself through cracks in the earth's surface.

This geological pot-pourri is echoed in the infinite variety of the British landscape. A few hundred miles from the flatness of the fenland, broken only by the spire of Ely Cathedral, you can explore the barren hills of the Peak District or go southwards and in a few hours drive to the hilly escarpments of the Chilterns.

Some of our countryside has been actively preserved through the hard work of the National Trust and the Countryside Commission. The South-West peninsular Coastal Path that runs over 500 miles from Minehead in Somerset to Poole Harbour in Dorset affords a splendid view of the Cornish coast, treacherous to ships, particularly in the 17th and 18th centuries when smuggling was rife and the wreckers, who would deliberately lure a ship to her doom by false signals, were terrifyingly active. The black rocks look as forbidding still and as dangerous, now the haunt of peregrine falcon and wheeling gulls.

A different type of wildness is to be found in the west by the heather and gorse covered moorland of Dartmoor and Exmoor. Little has changed here in the wilder parts. Iron Age man has left some trace of habitation, while modern man settles in the deep valleys carved out by old rivers.

Scotland, of course, has preserved large tracts of her landscape unchanged. Her vast lochs, often shrouded in mist which tumbles down the heatherclad mountainside, seem to have existed since the beginning of time. Wales too has her wilder spots but also a gentler beauty, the Brecon Beacons are more rounded and more accessible to farming, if not occupation, than the forbidding terrain of the Scottish highlands.

The early settlers coming from Europe occupied the south of England, pushing the previous inhabitants gradually north and west and farming the rich fertile areas of the lowlands. Sussex downland, perfect grazing for sheep, runs down from the coast into the Weald which was once entirely wooded. Continuous settlement has changed the face of the land, hedges separating fields of corn or grazing pasture have created a patchwork interrupted by villages and outlying farms.

This variety, some of it natural and the rest man–made, is our personal treasure, important to each one of us. The world is changing so fast that we must strive to preserve our natural heritage for ourselves and our children.

The Seven Sisters form part of the chain of white cliffs which run along the Kent and Sussex coast.

Far left:
Much of our countryside still bears evidence of earlier farming such as the open-field system originated by the Saxons at Laxton in Nottinghamshire.

Left:
Fogatt Edge rears forbiddingly out of the magnificent landscape of the Peak District, the first National Park to be declared in England.

Centre:
Ely's cathedral, once isolated on an island in the middle of the fens, still towers over the flat and now-drained marshland.

Bottom:
The setting sun illuminates part of the vast expanse of Lake Windermere, one of the most beautiful areas of the Lake District.

Top left:
Bowerman's Nose, a weathered piece of granite, looks sightlessly over to Devons rolling hills and patchwork of fields.

Left:
The bleakness of the scrub landscape of Dartmoor is legendary, suitable only to sustain grazing sheep.

Above:
The coast of Cornwall is a perilous one, especially Lands End where black cliffs jut forbiddingly into the Atlantic swell.

Right:
The New Forest in Hampshire reminds us that once most of Southern England was once thickly forested.

Right:
The fierce torrent of the river Llugwy creates Swallow Falls, one of three near Betwys-s-coed in Snowdonia.

Far right:
Kilchurn Castle on Loch Awe in Argyll seems dwarfed by the encroaching mountains and vastness of the loch.

Below:
Snowdonia, another of our National Parks is a wild and strangely beautiful terrain.

Left:
The Sussex landscape spreads out from the rolling downland into the rich grazing pastures and arable land of the Weald and beyond.

Far left:
The Broads, a network of linked lakes and rivers bordered with reeds cover nearly 5000 acres of the Norfolk countryside.

Centre:
The Quantock hills look out from North Somerset to the Bristol Channel. The beauty of this landscape enchanted the Romantic poets Wordsworth and Coleridge.

Below:
Landscape also exists beneath the ground. The Cheddar Gorge contains Aladdins caves of great beauty which have taken millenia to form.

Chapter 2

Monuments of Our Ancient Past

ritain is a land of legend, of magic, mystery and buried treasure. This is no more clearly shown than by the enormous variety of ancient sites which date back to the Bronze Age and beyond.

Perhaps the richest area is that of Wiltshire. From the downs near Marlborough looms Silbury Hill, the largest man-made prehistoric mound in Europe. Legend held it that a golden mounted horseman was buried deep in the centre but recent archaeological excavations have revealed nothing and Silbury remains mysterious still.

Avebury lies close by. An enormous megalithic monument of two stone circles surrounded by a third and circumscribed by a huge earthern bank. Like Stonehenge, Avebury has been thought to be anything from a druidic sun temple to an astronomical clock, aligned to the stars by precise mathematical formulae.

During the building of these two great sites other works were being constructed. Neolithic man buried his dead in earthern long barrows, then ones of stone, until by Bronze Age times round barrows started to dot the landscape. The Normanton barrow group in Wiltshire belongs to the latter type. The Bush Barrow yielded up various treasures, all of which illustrate the wealth of the Bronze Age culture of the time.

Prehistoric man also built houses to protect families and livestock. The village of Skara Brae in the Orkneys was rediscovered this century after 4000 years of concealment under sand, giving an intimate insight into the lives of a hardy group of colonists. The brochs or wheelhouses of Scotland are thought to be fortified farmhouses, though legends have it they are associated with fairy folk. Cornwall too has its share of Iron Age settlements like the village of Carn Euny which, in common with others of its type, boasts a fougous, a walled underground chamber running separate from the main village.

The Romans built their villas of varying sizes and magnificence. Perhaps one of the best appointed was that of Fishbourne near Chichester in Sussex with its splendid mosaics. But the rich could not have enjoyed the pleasures of civilisation were it not for Hadrians Wall, running from Wallsend-on-Tyne in the west to the Solway Firth in the east, patrolled by Roman legionaries to keep the fearsome Picts at bay. In late Roman times Pevensey Castle formed part of the ring of Saxon Shore

Forts built to protect the east and southern coasts from attack. The Roman Empire was crumbling and by 410 AD the Emperor Honorius had ordered an official retreat from the land his forebears had tamed and occupied for over four centuries.

Then came the Dark Ages and the slow struggle back to civilisation. All the aspirations of that black period seem enshrined in the famous deeds of King Arthur, his Knights of the Round Table and the power of his magician Merlin. With the Mediaeval period came the blossoming of Romanesque and Gothic architecture and the monastic art of illumination.

Like many church sites, that of Old Sarum, Wiltshire, completed in 1078 is built on an earlier hillfort. Today, as our population expands, we too are building on earlier sites and thus creating further layers of history. Some of those layers seem so distant in time that to our immediate ancestors they became the stuff of legend and dream.

Stonehenge, the finest Bronze Age sanctuary in Europe has been in existence for nearly 4000 years and still continues to fascinate us.

Above:
Silbury Hill stands 130 feet high above the surrounding Wiltshire countryside. Archaeologists have dated it to 2750 B.C. but its purpose is still an enigma.

Right:
The Uffington White Horse hillfigure in Berkshire has like others been stylistically attributed to the Iron Age. But for what purpose was it carved?

Far right:
Avebury village stands inside the largest megalithic monument in the country, even older in date than Stonehenge.

Left:
The Bronze Age Normanton Down barrow group is said to be the work of the wealthy 'Wessex' culture who had extensive trading links with Europe.

Below:
Skara Brae in the Orkneys is a wonderfully preserved Neolithic settlement. You can still see wall-cupboards, furniture and a sophisticated drainage system, all of stone.

Right:
These gold lozenges form part of the treasure excavated from the Bush Barrow, one of the Normanton group. It must have been the tomb of a great Wessex chieftain.

Bottom right:
Fougous, such as this one at Carn Euny, a Cornish Iron age village, are mysterious underground passages, perhaps built for storage or protection.

Above:
Maiden Castle, a gigantic Iron-Age hillfort, was eventually conquered by the Romans in the first century AD.

Top right:
Old Sarum is an ancient site which maintained its importance for many centuries. Originally a hillfort, it later boasted a Norman castle and a cathedral church.

Centre right:
Fishbourne was probably the palace of a local chief friendly to Rome. The mosaics are of high standard, like all the other appointments of the villa.

Right:
The famous broch of Mousa in the Shetlands is one of 500 similar dwellings found only in Scotland.

Left:

73 miles long, Hadrians wall protected the South from the Picts for nearly three centuries. It is the most enduring monument of the Roman occupation.

Far left:

The auxiliaries who guarded the Wall might well have been paid in some of these Roman coins dating from the third and fourth centuries AD.

Bottom left:

Merchants and soldiers alike worshipped the Persian deity Mithras. This sculpture of the birth of the god comes from Carrawburgh on Hadrians Wall.

Below:
Tintagel castle, perched on the rocky Cornish coastline is said to be where King Arthur was born late in the 5th century to Uther Pendragon, King of the Britons.

Bottom right:
Once strategically important to the Romans and later to William the Conqueror as a sea fort, Pevensey castle now stands guard over a silted-up harbour.

Right:
Originally founded in 635 AD Lindisfarne Priory was destroyed in the 9th century by the Danes. It was re-established two hundred years later as a Benedictine monastery.

Far right:
This cave, nestling at the foot of the cliff that bears Tintagel Castle, is reputed to be the cave of the magician Merlin.

Chapter 3

Splendid Buildings and Towns of Distinction

he establishment of Mediaeval culture laid the foundation of the Britain we know today. Cathedral cities such as York and London grew up through extensive trading links with Europe. Accumulated wealth was spent on endowing monasteries, building churches, castles and splendid homes and commissioning works of art and decoration, much of which we can still see today.

Greek and Latin classics were rediscovered and knowledge passed from the monasteries into towns and villages and led to the establishment of the University towns. Walking round the old colleges of Oxford and Cambridge, some granted their charters as early as 1380, you feel transported back to a more unhurried age, marked only by the bell on a clock tower and the sound of shoe leather on cobble as a student walks to a lecture.

Towns became established round centres of importance, of trade, learning and industry. Both Oxford and York, once the Viking capital of Jorvik, expanded to become great cathedral towns and important centres of the wool trade.

Smaller towns grew up, such as Rye, a thriving fishing village on the banks of the river Rother. A steep cobbled street still leads to the Mermaid Inn where smugglers two hundred years ago would store contraband goods in the cellars below.

Bath has a different charm, born of her elegant 18th century Nash terraces built during her heyday as a fashionable spa town. The Romans too knew of the curative properties of the waters and built a magnificent set of baths to take advantage of the healing spring.

The once glorious abbeys of Fountains, Rievaulx and Glastonbury are all ruins now, their treasures vanished. They once supported thriving colonies of monks who worked and grew fat on the land while dispensing alms to the poor – until the reign of Henry VIII; his assumption of the title 'Defender of the faith' with its rejection of Rome and the devastating final result – the Dissolution of the Monasteries.

There had always been trouble between church and state and the latter had never taken any chances. Castles dot the country such as Windsor, established by William the Conqueror, once Henry VIII's favourite residence and still popular with the Royal Family today.

His daughter, Princess Elizabeth, later to be crowned Elizabeth I in

Westminster Abbey spent her long confinement at Hatfield House. A later glorious redbrick Jacobean Palace was built in the grounds, one of the earliest of its kind, indicative of the movement from castle to stately home as the preferred residence of the noble and the wealthy.

Chatsworth still belongs to the Duke of Devonshire and like many mansions, is crammed with priceless jewels, paintings and furniture. Blenheim is an austerely splendid palace, its grandeur echoed in the formal gardens and the vastness of its man-made lake. Brighton Pavilion on the other hand, is light, airy, and colourful, with a fairytale exoticism.

Only a handful of our heritage in brick and stone can be mentioned and only a glimpse allowed of the treasures that are stored within. Every village, town or city has its own riches, all of which add something individual and unique to the fabric of our history.

Westminster Abbey has long been the place for both the coronation and burial of English monarchs.

Left:
This view into the quad of All Souls College amply justifies the description of Oxford as being 'a city of dreaming spires'.

Opposite Page:
Salisbury boasts the only English cathedral built as a single architectural conception; It was completed in 60 years after its foundation in 1220.

Bottom left:
The focus of Rye's smuggling past lies in the cellars of the Mermaid Inn, up a steep cobbled street of the same name.

Below:
Once a legionary fortress, York has grown in size and magnificence, the variety of her architecture bearing witness to the march of time.

Above:
The Romans dedicated a splendid classical temple at Bath to Sul and the Roman Minerva whose gilded bronze head was excavated from the baths.

Right:
The Romans called Bath Aquae Sulis after the local deity of the healing spring. Their splendid baths still remain incorporated into the 18th century Pump Room.

Top right:
Glastonbury Abbey, now in ruins, is intimately connected with the Grail Legends. King Arthur and his queen, Guinevere are said to have been buried here.

Bottom right:
Fountains Abbey has fallen into ruins since the Dissolution. The major part of this 300 foot cellarium was the lay brothers refectory.

Above:
The magnificent Jacobean mansion of Hatfield is enormous and impressive. It was built by Robert Cecil, 1st Earl of Salisbury in the early 17th century.

Top left:
Buckingham Palace was bought from a Duke of that name by George III. It has been the principal royal residence since the reign of Queen Victoria.

Centre left:
Stored in the Royal Mews at the rear of Buckingham Palace, the Gold State Coach has been used for every coronation since 1762.

Bottom left:
Windsor Castle has long been a favourite royal residence. It is also famous for the Garter Chapel and a magnificent art collection.

Left:
Once a monastery of the 12th century, this tide-encircled mansion has belonged to the St. Aubyn family for 300 years.

Far left:
The Prince Regent, later George IV, was so entranced with the resort of Brighthelmstone, now modern Brighton, that he built the Royal Pavilion.

Below left:
Blenheim Palace was constructed for the 1st Duke of Marlborough in gratitude for his military successes on the continent in the early 18th century.

Below:
The Duke of Marlborough's Cup forms part of the rich treasures on view at Blenheim Palace in Oxfordshire.

Chapter 4

Our Heritage from Prehistoric Times to the Elizabethan Age

very period in history has its own distinctive style which is echoed in the buildings and works of art of the time. Britain, from the earliest Celtic invasions to the reign of Good Queen Bess, has seen remarkable changes, much of which is reflected in her priceless treasures.

The Celts lived by the sword; believing it a great honour to die in battle, they lived life to the full. Their artistic skills lay in metalwork, chasing weapons and domestic objects with intricate interlacing designs such as seen on the Desborough mirror. The Anglo-Saxons, of Celtic stock themselves, loved complex designs, producing fine goldwork encrusted with precious stones. Like the Franks Casket with its runic inscription and Norse-influenced decoration, the Sutton Hoo treasure, which dates back to the 7th century AD clearly shows the Anglo-Saxon love of barbaric splendour.

Converted to Christianity, the Saxons built monasteries in which the monks followed the European example of manuscript illumination. The Lindisfarne Gospels show to perfection this love of abstract pattern and colour. Over the centuries that followed these monastic artists became increasingly confident in their representation of the human figure as shown by the Luttrell Psalter and the Alfred jewel.

The Romans, however, had been masters of the representation of the human form for centuries. The great silver dish from the Mildenhall silver hoard with its female musicians in swirling drapery dancing inside the rim is exquisite – obviously the prized possession of an important Roman official.

William the Conqueror finally brought stability to a country which had been in turmoil since the Romans departed. Sturdy castles and monasteries began to be built, their style determined by French and European influences. The Lewis Chessmen form part of this international style, called Romanesque. By the end of the 14th century Romanesque solidity has given way to the Gothic style with its soaring pinnacles and complex ornament, echoing the other-worldly aspirations of a people ruined by feudalism and decimated by the Black Death and the Crusades.

More than a century later Hans Holbein, Henry VIII's favourite artist, gives us an insight into the minds of the Tudors. His "Ambassadors" is a statement about the power, connections and splendour of the Tudor court. Another witness to Tudor wealth is the wreck of the *Mary Rose*, flagship of Henry's new fleet until a July day in 1545 when she sank in Portsmouth harbour with nearly all hands on board. Raised by a dedicated team of archaeologists, her wealth is to be counted in gold coin and the intimate details of Tudor life afforded by less precious objects.

Henry's daughter Elizabeth did not only make England feared on the high seas. She also fostered art and gracious living at home, from the plays of William Shakespeare to the intricate and delicate work of Nicolas Hilliard, the master miniaturist.

From the Celts to the Elizabethan court takes us through two thousand years of development and change. Magnificent works of art in our museums, galleries and churches bear mute but powerful testimony to the forces that shaped our history.

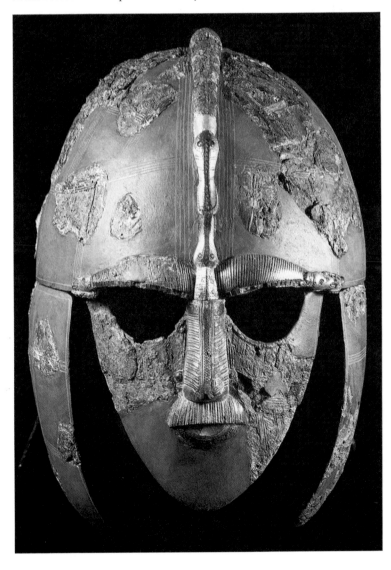

The Sutton Hoo helmet reconstructed from fragments, forms part of a spectacular array of Anglo-Saxon treasure now on public display in the British Museum.

41

Right:
The curvilinear designs on the back of the Desborough Mirror reveal the Celts as gifted and sensitive artists.

Centre right:
This photograph shows the excavated Sutton Hoo longship burial. No human remains were found with the treasure.

Far right:
This gold buckle from the Sutton Hoo treasure shows the Anglo-Saxon love of interlacing design, here of snakes and strange animals.

Below right:
This shoulder clasp from Sutton Hoo is a splendid piece of jewellery made from gold inlaid with garnets and mosaic glass.

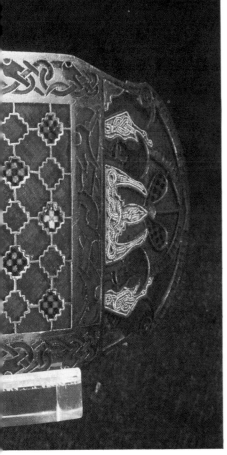

Left:
The Alfred Jewel commissioned by King Alfred, is thought to have originally served as a pointer attached to a rod for the reading of religious texts.

Bottom:
The Lewis Chessmen comprise 93 pieces – nearly four sets – all carved from walrus ivory. They are quite charming and at times even humorous.

Far left:
This beautiful great silver dish was buried with other treasures at Mildenhall in Suffolk to escape looting by Anglo-Saxon invaders.

Bottom:
The Franks casket from the late 7th century is made of whalebone and decorated with runes as well as pagan and Christian scenes.

Above:
This selection of personal items ranging from a rosary to a pocket sundial probably belonged to officers of the Mary Rose.

Top right:
This is a contemporary illustration of the Mary Rose, Henry VIII's flagship, sunk during a skirmish with the French in 1545, now on public display in Portsmouth.

Right:
The Wilton Diptych shows Richard II being presented to the Virgin and Child by two of his patron saints.

Right:
The Luttrell Psalter is famed for its charming evocation of daily life in 14th century England.

Bottom right:
This is the opening of St. Matthews Gospel from the Lindisfarne Gospels, one of the first and greatest masterpieces of mediaeval book illumination.

Far right:
Holbeins Two ambassadors are clearly men of culture wealth and standing in the Tudor court.

Below:
Nicholas Hilliard was famous in his own day for the delicacy of his miniatures. This portrait of an unknown youth is only 140 by 70 mm.

Chapter 5

Our Heritage from Charles I to the Age of Steam

s we move forward in time from the age of the Stuarts through to the Victorian epoch we can see the effect the gradual build-up and consolidation of empire had on the decorative arts of this country. It was also a period when we began to lead the world in invention, laying the cornerstones of a technology which affects the world today.

The reign of Charles I brought England into the centre of European politics. Painting was influenced by the Renaissance tradition which was to magnify the kingly virtues. Van Dyck was lured from Holland to paint the splendours of the English court. His magnificent equestrian portrait of Charles subtly portrays the majesty of the king and yet hints at the weakness of the man, a weakness which led to the scaffold.

Systematic destruction of the Crown Jewels occurred under Oliver Cromwell's protectorate. A new set were specially created for the coronation of Charles II which we can see today in the Jewel House at the Tower of London.

The Eighteenth century was a time of brilliance, wars, sophistication and new ideas. The arts flourished, moving from the imaginative flamboyance of Rococo design, tamed a little in the porcelain shepherdesses of the period, to the sterner lines of the Neo-classical. It was also the Age of Hogarth, his *Rakes Progress* is a cynical but accurate portrayal of the morality of the age. This morality was heavily criticised by William Blake in his mystical writings which he illustrated with symbolic figures of great power and skill.

The work of Stubbs leans away from comment towards a newfound interest in animals and nature. Constable went further continually experimenting, he tried to recreate nature with new immediacy. His famous *Haywain* contrasts with the more impressionistic work of his later years. Impressionism was taken to extraordinary and dramatic lengths by William Mallord Turner, perhaps the greatest painter we have produced.

We are reminded again of Britain's rank as premier maritime nation of the world by the *Victory*, Nelson's flagship at the Battle of Trafalgar and the scene of that great Admiral's death. As conqueror of the seas we established trade routes from the Channel to the China Seas. Cottons from India and Egypt were conveyed back to Lancashire where the raw materials were manufactured into garments in factories which utilised the first industrial machinery.

Britain led the world in the early years not only in the factories but in new engineering works. Isambard Kingdom Brunel built the first suspension bridge at Clifton in Bristol and the SS Great Britain, the first iron ship.

William Frith, another Victorian, painted the ordinary people of his time. Here we see the emergence of a new breed – the prosperous and respectable middle class who he paints as they appear in their finery at Epsom for Derby Day.

It was at the end of the 19th century, that there was a mild backlash. Some felt that the values of earlier times had been lost in a flood of materialism. One of these was William Morris, who founded the Pre-Raphaelite Brotherhood dedicated to the preservation of ancient crafts and the portrayal of a simpler life. They created furniture and decoration that contrasted with the heaviness of Victorian taste.

And thus we are brought full circle, reminded again of the necessity of preserving our cultural heritage. It is a continual reminder of the greatness of our past and an inspiration for the future.

Blake's unique style is well illustrated by The Ancient of Days, *depicting the Old Testament god creating the world with a pair of golden compasses.*

Left:
This charming Worcester porcelain group dates from 1770 and is typically Rococco in its carefree and asymmetrical design.

Below:
Van Dyck's huge painting, Charles I on Horseback *is the artist's most formal and magnificent portrait of the doomed king.*

Far left:
Painted in 1732, Hogarth's The Orgy *from his series entitled* The Rakes' Progress *depicts the debauched life-style of a young man about town.*

Below:
Stubbs is well-known for his extraordinarily accurate paintings of animals, particularly horses, all based on an intimate knowledge of anatomy.

Above:
William Frith's Derby Day *is a microcosm of Victorian society, ranging from the fashionable wealthy classes to impoverished gipsies.*

Above right:
Edward Burne-Jones and Dante Gabriel Rossetti, founder members of the Pre-Raphaelite Brotherhood designed these two stained glass windows.

Right:
One of William Morris' enduringly popular textile designs which are still manufactured by Libertys of London.

Far right:
Constable's most famous painting The Haywain *is of Flatford Mill in his beloved Suffolk. The area is now known as 'Constable country'.*

Left:
Turner's painting of the old Trafalgar veteran, The Fighting Temeraire, *being towed to her final berth becomes almost elegiac through his brushwork and subtle colouration.*

Far left:
HMS Victory, now in dry dock at Portsmouth was Nelson's flagship at Trafalgar, a victory which ensured our supremacy over Napoleon on the seas.

Below left:
On 21 October 1805 Nelson lay dying on the deck of his flagship. Maclise's painting gives some idea of the horror and chaos of battle at sea.

Below right:
The silver-gift Trafalgar Vase was commissioned to celebrate the British Naval victory. Britannia is pictured as a Herculean figure destroying the hydra-headed Napoleon.

Above:
All the regalia in this picture is used during the coronation. They include the eagle shaped ampulla and spoon for the ritual anointing of the new monarch.

Top right:
The Tower of London, originally a Roman fort and later a prison for traitors to the crown, now guards one of our most precious treasures – the Crown Jewels.

Bottom right:
Brunel's S.S. Great Britain was the first steam screw-propelled iron ship to cross the Atlantic – nearly 140 years ago.

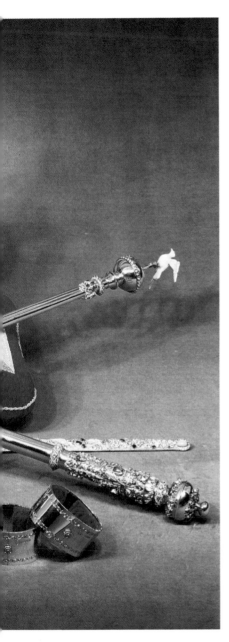

Chapter 6

Buried Treasure

he lure of buried treasure has acted as a magnet for mankind from early times. The Spanish conquistadors' search for Eldorado, the fabled land of gold and the perennial eagerness of the public to flock to glittering exhibitions of archaeological treasures all bear witness to a deep-seated fascination with the subject.

However, if you are a budding treasure hunter, there are important legal points of which you must be aware. The term Treasure Trove applies only to gold and silver which has been buried with the intention of recovery. Thus the Snettisham torc, an exquisite piece of Celtic craftmanship made from twisted wires of electrum, a gold and silver alloy, was declared treasure trove as it was considered by the coroner to be deliberately concealed, and so reverted to the crown. However, the finder not the landowner is paid the market price by the Crown for the object as a reward.

If, on the other hand, treasure has been buried as grave goods (such as the Sutton Hoo finds) or if it has been lost, then ownership reverts to whoever holds the land in which the objects are found.

Before you invest in a metal detector (a fairly expensive item) and a spade, you must remember that every piece of land in this country is under individual or group ownership and subject to various restrictions, while some areas are strictly forbidden to treasure hunters. If the area you have selected does not fall into these categories you must still approach the owner and secure his permission, otherwise various legal actions are open to him.

Should you, despite the above mentioned hazards, discover say a Tudor Silver Shilling, having made arrangements with the owner of the land, the next step is to report your find to the police. In this instance it is unlikely that a single coin has been buried deliberately and this will not be declared Treasure Trove.

However a Tudor shilling is not just intrinsically valuable, it can also help archaeologists and local historians to fit another piece into the jigsaw of local history. Responsible treasure hunters should remember the exact location of their find and take it in to their local museum or archaeological society for examination and record.

Perhaps the best way of treasure hunting (with none of the strictures of local bye-laws and other legal complexities) is to sign on for a local archaeological excavation or 'dig'. You then gradually begin to interpret history with the eyes of the archaeologist, learning that any object uncovered is equally important in terms of the context in which it is found.

Construction work, whether of new buildings or roads is wiping out evidence of Britain's past faster than 'Rescue' digs can be mobilised. It is therefore up to each one of us, whether treasure hunter or interested observer, to be responsible for our actions. Without such a sense we are allowing information essential to our comprehension of our island history to be lost forever.

This coin hoard forms part of a display illustrating trade in Mediaeval London. Each piece of evidence helps archaeologists towards a greater knowledge of the past.

Right:

This beautifully chased Celtic Ceremonial shield, found near the Thames at Battersea, is made of bronze and does not fall into the category of Treasure Trove.

Far right:

The Snettisham torc, a Celtic neck ornament, formed part of the hoards of metalwork found around the Norfolk village of that name.

Centre:

The Water Newton treasure of Christian silver, of which this magnificent jug forms a part, was discovered by an amateur archaeologist only a decade ago.

Below right:

These silver plaques are early Christian votive offerings from the Water Newton hoard. Declared Treasure Trove, they are now in the British Museum.

Photographic Acknowledgements

The Ashmolean Museum, Oxford: 45 *top*.
Janet and Colin Bord: 6–7 *bottom centre*, 12 *bottom*, 17 *bottom left*, 21, 23 *bottom*, 24, 25 *top & bottom*, 35 *top*, 36 *top*.
Bridgeman Art Library; The Bible Society: 48 *bottom right*; Blenheim Palace: 39 *bottom right*; British Library: 48 *top*; British Museum: 26 *top*, 44 *top*; Museum of London: 2; Royal Worcester: 53 *top*; The Trustees of The Sir John Soane Museum: 52 *top*; The Tate Gallery, London: 54 top; Victoria and Albert Museum: 481, 55 *top*, 57 *bottom*.
Courtesy of the Trustees of the British Museum: 42 *top left & top right*, 45 *bottom*, 62-3.
British Tourist Authority: 6–7 *top left, top right*, 11 *bottom*, 15, 17 *bottom right*, 20 *top*, 28, 29 *top*, 33 *bottom right*, 35 *bottom*, 36 *centre & bottom*, 39 *bottom left*, 60.
Crown Copyright. Reproduced with the permission of the Controller of Her Majesty's Stationery Office: 22 *top*, 58–59.
Susan Griggs Agency; Rob Cousins: 11 *top*, 13 *bottom*; Anthony Howarth: 20 *bottom*; Robert McFarlane: 17 *top*, Michael St Maur Sheil: 14; Ted Spiegel: 10; Adam Woolfitt: 5,9,13 *top*, 16, 22 *bottom*, 28-9 *bottom*, 34, 39 *top*.
Hamlyn Picture Library: 12 *top*, 33 *bottom left*, 54 *bottom*, 59 *top*.
Michael Holford: 19, 25 *centre*, 26 *bottom*, 32, 34 *right*, 37, 38; British Museum: 41, 42 *bottom*, 43, 44 *bottom*, 51.
Mary Rose Trust: 46, 47 *top*.
Reproduced by courtesy of the Trustees of the National Gallery, London: 47 *bottom*, 49, 53 *bottom*, 55 *bottom*, 56-7 *top right*.
David Parker: 27.
Spectrum Colour Library: 6–7 *bottom right*, 11 *centre*, 29 *bottom*, 31, 33 *top*, 59 *bottom*, 56 *top*.
The Tate Gallery, London: 52 *bottom*.
Walker Art Gallery, Liverpool: 56 *bottom*.
The Wiltshire Archaeological and Natural History Society: 23 *top*.